A SHORT BIOGRAPHY OF JACQUELINE KENNEDY

A SHORT BIOGRAPHY OF
Jacqueline Kennedy

Mim Harrison

BENNA BOOKS

Carlisle, Massachusetts

A Short Biography of Jacqueline Kennedy

Series Editor: Susan DeLand
Written by: Mim Harrison

Copyright © 2017 Applewood Books, Inc.

978-1-944038-30-4

Front cover: *Jacqueline Bouvier Kennedy,* 1970
Aaron Shikler, Oil on canvas
27.8 cm x 42.22 cm
White House Collection / White House Historical Association
Back cover: *First Lady Jacqueline Kennedy and her children*
John F. Kennedy Jr. and Caroline Kennedy riding, 1962
Cecil Stoughton White House Photographs,
John F. Kennedy Presidential Library and Museum, Boston
ST-498-1-62

Published by Benna Books
an imprint of Applewood Books, Inc.
Carlisle, Massachusetts

To request a free copy of our current catalog
featuring our best-selling books, write to:
Applewood Books
P.O. Box 27
Carlisle, Massachusetts 01741
Or visit us on the web at: www.awb.com

10 9 8 7 6 5 4 3 2 1
MANUFACTURED IN THE UNITED STATES OF AMERICA

JACQUELINE KENNEDY DESCRIBED her husband, President John Fitzgerald Kennedy, as "elusive" and "unforgettable." These words could also describe Jackie. As the First Lady of America's thirty-fifth president, Jacqueline Kennedy was an extraordinarily private person living in a relentlessly curious public eye. She is remembered for her commitment to history, demonstrated in her restoration of the White House; her elevation of a cultured life, bringing artists of all kinds into the executive mansion and to the national forefront; and her nearly faultless sense of style.

Jacqueline Lee Bouvier was born on July 28, 1929, in Southampton on Long Island, New York. Lee was the maiden name of her mother, Janet, who was sixteen years younger than her husband, John Vernou Bouvier III. Like JFK (who was twelve years older than Jackie), he was also called Jack—most famously, "Black Jack," for his handsome dark features.

The Bouviers and the Lees both had homes on Park Avenue in New York and in the Hamptons on Long Island, but they were not fond of one another. The Bouviers traced their lineage to southern France; the Lees, to Ireland. This was a time when the difference mattered. Regardless, Jackie's paternal grandfather favored her among his many grandchildren. He loved poetry, something Jackie was drawn to at an early age, writing her own poems when she was just ten. Jackie, in turn, adored her father, despite his penchant for gambling, drink, and women. Her sister, Caroline Lee Bouvier, was born four years after Jackie. She was always

The Lees were arrivistes in the eyes of the longer-settled Bouviers.

known as Lee; years later, Jackie named her daughter Caroline for her sister.

The family summered in the Hamptons and lived the rest of the time on Park Avenue. The girls took ballet classes. Jackie attended Miss Chapin's—the Chapin School for Girls. She was known as pretty and precocious and frequently inclined to schoolgirl mischief. Jackie's teacher, Miss Platt, described her as "a darling child, very clever, very artistic, and full of the devil."

Despite the trappings of privilege, life was not particularly serene. Money was a constant worry after Black Jack's wealth fell victim to the stock market crash of October 1929—just a few months after Jackie was born. Jack's womanizing became increasingly untenable for his wife, and they divorced in 1940. Janet remarried in June 1942 to Hugh D. Auchincloss Jr. Nicknamed "Hughdie," he possessed a considerable fortune as an heir to the monstrously wealthy Standard Oil Company. Jackie and Lee's orbit now tilted; the family lived most of the year at his Merrywood estate in McLean, Virginia, and summered at his other estate, Hammersmith Farm in Newport, Rhode Island.

Jackie's father was not the only colorful character in the family. His sister, Edith Bouvier Beale, known as "Big Edie," and her daughter, "Little Edie," were eccentric recluses living in their mansion in the Hamptons called Grey Gardens and subjects of the documentary of the same name. Jackie had food and clothing delivered to them throughout her life.

Jackie was a lifelong Francophile, learning French at an early age (and later Latin and Spanish). As a child she had a poodle, which she named Gaullie, after France's Charles de Gaulle. The French returned the admiration when she was First Lady. She was greeted so warmly during her 1961 trip to France that her husband, President Kennedy, famously joked that he was "the man who accompanied Jacqueline Kennedy to Paris." But Jackie had already made de Gaulle, by then presi-

Like both her parents, Jackie was an accomplished horsewoman. When her pony tossed her in a horse show as a youngster, unfazed, she got back on.

dent of France, an admirer, after he had visited Washington the year before. "If there were anything I would take back to France with me," he said almost wistfully, "it would be Mrs. Kennedy."

Jackie's first trip to Washington was in 1941, as a tourist. She visited the White House, which did not impress her, and Arlington Cemetery, which did. Three years later, Jackie was packed off to the famously strict Miss Porter's School in Farmington, Connecticut. She excelled in literature and loved her theater courses. She drew whimsical cartoons for the school paper and wrote earnest essays on the French Enlightenment's effect on America. When she finished at Miss Porter's in 1947, she had her coming-out party as a debutante at Hammersmith. The society pages crowned her "Queen Debutante" of the year.

With her father's good looks and her stepfather's entrée into moneyed society, Jackie embarked for Europe the following summer. The "queen" went through the

Not surprisingly for someone who was developing a deep appreciation for the past, she enjoyed the Smithsonian's National Museum of American History.

receiving line at Buckingham Palace two times, in order to see her hero Winston Churchill twice. In Paris, she studied at the Sorbonne, mastering the French language. She stayed abroad for more than a year, traveling throughout Europe.

"I loved it more than any year of my life," she once wrote about her first trip abroad.

Jackie had enrolled at Vassar in the States. But after the grandness of Europe, returning to sleepy Poughkeepsie and Vassar seemed too small. Instead, she decided to study at George Washington University in Washington, D.C.

She entered an annual competition that Vogue magazine held called Prix de Paris. The winner received a six-month stint working in the Vogue office in Paris and another six months in its New York office. Jackie's essay was awash with the names of cultural icons she most wanted to meet: French poet Charles Baudelaire, the Irish novelist and dramatist Oscar Wilde, and cultural icon ballet impresario Sergei Diaghilev. Jackie won the contest, leaving more than twelve hundred other applicants in the dust.

Jackie then embarked for Europe again, with her sister in tow, wearing clothes she designed herself. The two charmed their way through England, France, Italy, and Spain, where one of Jackie's favorite books, *The Sun Also Rises* by Ernest Hemingway, came alive.

This time, when Jackie returned to the States, even *Vogue,* the grand dame of fashion magazines, seemed too small. She did not complete her six months at the New York office. Instead, she returned to George Washington University, studying French literature. She got a job as "Inquiring Photographer" for the *Washington Times-Herald* newspaper. One of the intriguing questions she often posed was, "When did you discover that women are not the weaker sex?"

Powerful men attracted her. Even so, the first time she met Jack Kennedy at a dinner party hosted by Charlie Bartlett, a mutual friend, and his wife, nothing much came of it. Another admirer was waiting for Jackie outside in the car. Undaunted,

Lee and Jackie wrote a diary together, which Jackie whimsically illustrated, and they presented it to their mother as a gift. It remains a popular book called *One Special Summer.*

Even though Lee was often considered the prettier of the two Bouvier girls, Jackie conveyed a mystique.

Charlie held another dinner party on May 8, 1952, and invited the two again. This time, they clicked.

They were both extraordinarily attractive. A slender and graceful five feet seven, Jackie possessed her father's dark good looks, with dark eyes set beguilingly far apart. Jack Kennedy was tall at six feet and undeniably handsome: thick auburn hair, intense blue eyes, and a self-assured smile. At age thirty-five, he exuded the charisma that would later captivate a nation and much of the world.

News of JFK's heroics were splashed all over the American media, from *Reader's Digest* to the *New Yorker*.

Kennedy was a war hero, receiving the Purple Heart during World War II for heroics following the sinking of PT-109, the boat that he skippered. A Japanese destroyer bore down upon the boat off the coast of the Solomon Islands and Kennedy rescued most of the men. He kept the men alive for a harrowing six days until they were found on one of the islands. Kennedy used a coconut shell to carve out a message for the naval command. "ALIVE," it announced, "NAURO ISL / NA-

IVE KNOWS POSIT / HE CAN PILOT / 11 ALIVE NEED SMALL BOAT / KENNEDY" Kennedy gave the message to two native islanders, who paddled thirty-five miles in a canoe to the nearest Allied military base. A rescue boat brought PT-109's crew to safety.

After returning to the States, this war hero successfully entered politics. Kennedy was in the House of Representatives when Jackie met him, already planning a run for the Senate.

Jackie and Jack were both smart and witty. Jack was as well read as Jackie—and loved poetry. They both admired Churchill. They were intellectual equals, Jackie providing Jack with important insight when he translated numerous books in French addressing the politics of Southeast Asia.

Jackie often recited one of JFK's favorite poems to him, the eerily prescient "I Have a Rendezvous with Death," by Alan Seeger.

"Maybe it will end very happily— or maybe since he's this old and set in his ways and cares so desperately about his career he just won't want to give up that much time to extra-curricular things like marrying me!"

Jack was smitten and proposed in early May 1953. Perhaps to consider her answer, Jackie sailed to Europe on an ocean liner but flew back to Boston, and Kennedy was there to meet her. They announced their engagement on June 24.

Kennedy's father, Joseph, the hyper-ambitious Irishman from Boston who had made his family multimillionaires, thought Jackie was the perfect choice of wife for the son he expected to be president.

St. Mary's Roman Catholic Church in Newport, Rhode Island, where they were married on September 12, 1953, could hold only about seven hundred fifty people. Fortunately, the sprawling oceanfront estate at nearby Hammersmith Farm could easily accommodate the more than one thousand guests who attended the reception. "Black Jack" Bouvier was not one of them. Nor had he given his daughter away at the church: he was too inebriated. Hughdie did, instead.

Jackie was now officially part of the

Jackie's veil had been her maternal grandmother's. Lee, already married, was her matron of honor. Bobby Kennedy was Jack's best man.

Kennedy clan—big, boisterous, intensely competitive. She remained aloof from much of that, and did what she could to keep her husband in her quiet, intellectual orbit. The summer before, when they were staying with his family on Cape Cod, she had even persuaded Kennedy to paint with her.

Though she preferred Proust over politics, she took courses in political science at Georgetown University. She went to the opening session of Congress in 1954 to be there with Jack. When her husband put in long days at his Senate office, which he often did, she would bring him lunch.

No brown paper bags for these lunches—they arrived on covered china.

In October 1954 Jack underwent a high-risk operation for his chronic and severe back pain that put him into a coma. The situation was grim enough that a priest administered last rites. He recovered, only to undergo another back surgery the following spring. Jackie stacked books by his bedside and read to him during his recovery. During this time, Jack began work on his book *Profiles in Cour-*

age, which would win a Pulitzer Prize. In the book's acknowledgments, he thanked his wife— "whose help during all the days of my convalescence, I cannot ever adequately acknowledge."

Both Jack and Jackie were worldlier than most Americans at that time, having spent time abroad. Jack lived in England for a time, in his youth, when his father had been U.S. ambassador to Great Britain in the late 1930s. In the late 1950s when Jack and Jackie were visiting friends in the south of France, they were invited to board a yacht owned by Aristotle Onassis named the *Christina.* Winston Churchill, now a somewhat frail octogenarian and no longer Britain's prime minister was a guest on the shipping magnate's private yacht. Kennedy went to meet his hero, Churchill, but Churchill barely acknowledged him. Jack laughed it off. "I think he thought I was the waiter," he said. Years later, on April 9, 1963, President John F. Kennedy made Churchill an honorary U.S. citizen.

On November 27, 1957, happiness came when their daughter Caroline was born. Jackie had earlier delivered a still-born baby girl whose name was to be Arabella. There had also been a miscarriage. For Jackie, the birth of Caroline was a cherished moment. Always protective of her children's privacy, Jackie made a major concession when she allowed *Life* magazine to shoot photographs of baby Caroline in 1958, in her parents' home. Jackie shared their family life with the public and the endearing photographs would help Jack get reelected to the Senate.

Caroline was christened in St. Patrick's Cathedral in New York, wearing her mother's christening gown.

"If you bungle raising your children, I don't think whatever else you do matters very much."

Jackie was a talented strategist and put this to good use when her husband announced, on January 2, 1960, that he was running for president of the United States. That winter, Jackie traveled with Jack on the campaign trail through a dozen states, even though she knew she was pregnant again. Her facility with other languages was always an asset. In Milwaukee, she spoke in Polish when telling a primarily Polish audience that "Poland will live forever." In Louisiana, she spoke to the Cajuns in French. She taped political ads in French, Spanish, and Italian.

When she did eventually have to curtail her campaign stumping as her pregnancy progressed, Jackie became "Campaign Wife," the author of a syndicated newspaper column that had echoes of Eleanor Roosevelt's column as First Lady, "My Day." The first installment of Jackie's "Campaign Wife" column ran September 19, 1960.

Jackie used the column in part to quell the kerfuffle about her glamorous, sophisticated clothes. She simply enjoyed what every woman did, she implied, when she described "the universal feminine sport of shopping." But Jackie used "Campaign Wife" as a much broader platform, writing at one point of how she would "always be

Privately, she reconnected with *Vogue* magazine, asking the editor-in-chief for suggestions on how to counter the impression that she was a walking billboard for French couture. Diana Vreeland's advice: "Buy American."

grateful to politics for showing me America." It was not a hollow statement. When Jackie became First Lady, she purchased new glassware for the White House from factories in West Virginia. She had seen firsthand during the campaign the area's grinding poverty. Perhaps most significantly, she used the column to encourage women to articulate their concerns about the issues of the day.

Jackie joined her husband for his third televised debate against Republican opponent Richard Nixon on October 13, in New York. A few days later, she sat in the back of an open convertible with JFK for a rousing ticker-tape parade through Spanish Harlem.

> *"The one thing I do not want to be called is First Lady. It sounds like a saddle horse."*

"Oh, Bunny, you're president!" Those were Jackie's first words to her husband as president-elect, on election night, November 8. It was a tad premature—both went to bed before Nixon formally conceded. Jackie's baby was also premature. John Jr. was expected in December but arrived on November 25.

Jackie convalesced at the Kennedy home in Palm Beach. While JFK worked on his inaugural address, she read and planned for what would become her major work at the White House, restoring the rooms to their history.

But first would be her presentation to the world at the inaugural festivities. She chose as her clothing designer Oleg Cassini, an ideal hybrid for her of a European who lived in America. Cassini created her gown for the ball the night before the inauguration ceremony. Ball gowns are meant to be breathtaking, but equally so was the ensemble that Cassini designed for the inauguration ceremony itself—a simple but stylishly cut light tan coat with fur-trimmed collar, a matching pillbox hat, and the inspired addition of a sable muff. From day one, the First Lady was setting

Jackie designed her own gown for the Inaugural Ball.

a new level of understated elegance in fashion.

> *"All these people come to see the White House and they see practically nothing that dates back before 1948."*

Jackie had demonstrated her penchant, and talent, for decorating the homes that she and Kennedy lived in. At one point, she had redecorated the rooms in their Georgetown home, this time in a monotone of light tan. A mildly exasperated Jack Kennedy had turned to his mother-in-law, who was visiting, and said, "Mrs. Auchincloss, do you think we're prisoners of beige?"

But Jacqueline Kennedy's redo of the White House rooms was not a redecoration. It was a restoration of the storied mansion's history. The interior was uninspired, its last facelift being during Truman's tenure, when the ever-frugal Harry bought department-store furnishings. (In his defense, he'd had to spend a considerable sum to rebuild the mansion's entire structure, which was in danger of literally falling apart.) Jackie said, "It must be restored—and that has nothing to do with decoration. That is a question of scholarship."

Years later, Caroline Kennedy recalled one of Jackie's best friends relating how, shortly after the election, Jackie bemoaned to her, "We have to live in that huge house, with all those curtains."

Jackie's passion for historical authenticity was unabating. She told a reporter for *Time*, "I would write fifty letters to fifty museum curators if I could bring Andrew Jackson's inkwell home."

To make up for what she knew would be a dearth of congressional funds, she created the Committee of the Fine Arts Commission for the White House, with an A-list of members as long as its name. Henry E. du Pont, the country's leading authority on American decorative arts and the committee's chair, was charged

In undertaking the restoration, Jackie was in some ways following in the footsteps of Mary Todd Lincoln, who had orchestrated a major do-over in her day.

ith tracking down and acquiring—often through donations—authentic period ieces. Jackie's billionaire friend Bunny Mellon, of the Listerine fortune, was a ommittee member and redesigned the Rose Garden. Charles Adams, whose ancestor John Adams had been the first resident to live in the White House, also served on the committee. The major media of the day—*Life, Time, Look,* the *Saturday Evening Post*—all reported favorably on the renovation and helped to give American readers a sense of ownership in he Blue Room, the Red Room, the Green Room, the Treaty Room, the East Room, he State Dining Room, and the Lincoln Bedroom. Jackie then cemented that with er televised tour of the newly restored White House on February 14, 1962. It enerated ten thousand fan letters.

But she wasn't finished. She wanted a guidebook on the restoration that would ppeal to young people, and so she established the White House Historical Association to serve as publisher. Jackie was

A special legislative act protected the committee's acquisitions as "property of the White House," assigning the Smithsonian as the caretaker of objects not on display.

hands-on in her oversight of the guide. A one point, she noted that the book's intro duction should have a "marvelous closin sentence worthy of Euripides."

Her love of the arts filled the Whit House with music, theater, and dance— concert by the cellist Pablo Casals, the Yo Yo Ma of his day; the actor Basil Rathbon of Sherlock Holmes fame reading Elizabe than poetry; the American Ballet Theatr performing for the president of Africa' Côte d'Ivoire. (Jackie made sure the pro gram was printed in French.)

By early 1963, Jackie was expectin another child. On August 9, 1963, John Kennedy had to break the news to hi wife, in the hospital recovering from th Caesarean delivery: their two-day-ol son, Patrick, born prematurely, had die of respiratory distress syndrome. A shat tered Jackie retreated from the public eye for weeks, taking a recuperative cruise through the Mediterranean that Octobe on a private yacht. She was the guest o Aristotle Onassis. It was only the second me Jackie met him, but her sister, now Princess Radziwill, had frequently been n Onassis' company over the years. When Lee told him about Patrick's death, Onassis suggested Jackie take refuge on the *Christina*.

By that November, Jackie felt sufficiently restored to accompany her husband on his reelection campaign trips to Texas, including one to Dallas on November 22. Riding in a motorcade through the streets of the city, her husband, President John F. Kennedy, was assassinated. The last image America has of the couple is of the First Lady frantically trying to climb out of the back seat of the open car she and JFK were in, in a desperate attempt to get help for her husband. He had been shot, first in the neck and then in the head, and just moments earlier had collapsed into her lap, with a portion of his skull exposed and a blood-splattered Jackie crying, "I love you, Jack."

In Washington the next day, she gathered her two small children and had them

She refused to change out of her bloodied pink suit for the swearing-in aboard Air Force One of her husband's successor, Vice President Lyndon B. Johnson.

both write a letter to their deceased father, which Jackie added to her own before JFK's casket was closed.

> *"Now, I think that I should have known that he was magic all along. I did know it—but I should have guessed that it would be too much to ask to grow old with and see our children grow up together. So now, he is a legend when he would have preferred to be a man."*

The most devastating hours of Jacqueline Kennedy's life were her finest hour as First Lady. The funeral of John F. Kennedy which she directed the following Monday was both personal and magisterial—the Black Watch pipers; the incessant, somber drumbeats; the riderless horse bearing the symbolic reversed boots; Jackie's unfathomable poise walking behind the gun carriage that carried her husband's casket.

The Arlington Cemetery that Jackie had admired as a young girl was now he

Among the heads of state following behind Jackie was French President Charles de Gaulle.

husband's final resting place, a single basket of flowers from the Rose Garden at the gravesite, the Eternal Flame waiting for her to ignite it.

Earlier that month, in anticipation of Veterans Day, Jackie had taught her little boy how to salute. As JFK's casket passed his children and widow on the way to the cemetery, Jackie leaned down and spoke to her son. John Jr., who had just turned three years old that day, made the final, poignant gesture of farewell for his family: a heartbreakingly perfect military salute to his hero.

As deeply as the nation mourned, for Jacqueline Kennedy the grieving was almost unbearable. She sought, with little success, some solace in reading *The Greek Way* by Edith Hamilton, looking to the ancient Greeks—Euripides among them—for answers on human suffering. Years later, observers would come to believe that she had suffered from the same posttraumatic stress disorder, or PTSD, in witnessing the violent death of her

Months after her husband's death, with special permission, Jackie had the remains of her two deceased children, Arabella and Patrick, moved and buried beside their father.

husband that combat soldiers do. Many of the telltale signs were there—months of sleeplessness, years of being fearful, a near compulsion to relive and relate the grisly, gruesome details again and again.

But her legacy transcends that agony. To Jackie Kennedy, the country owed not only the stately show of homage following a senseless assassination, but also the myth of Camelot that grew up around JFK's presidency. Before November 1963 drew to a close, Jackie had related Jack's affection for the fable to the journalist and historian Theodore White, who shared it with the country on the pages of *Life* magazine. It is because of this that admirers who lived through the Kennedy presidency often recall it as the "one brief shining moment" of Camelot.

JFK's brother Bobby was assassinated in Los Angeles on June 5, 1968, and Jackie Kennedy lost the man who had looked out for her and her children since his brother's death. Vulnerable and traumatized all over again, and fearing for her children's safety,

Kennedy had loved the musical *Camelot* just as he had loved reading about Arthur and the Round Table as a child.

hat fall she moved her family to Greece and married the stunningly wealthy Aristotle Onassis, thirty years her senior. He had been a family acquaintance of many years, and five years earlier had attended JFK's funeral, paying his respects to the widow in the White House and offering support.

Onassis was one of the world's richest men, worth a reported $500 million. Though often described as a Greek shipping magnate, he was born in Turkey. A self-made multimillionaire, Onassis controlled dozens of companies, most notably ships, in different countries. For several decades, he also owned Olympic Airways.

In addition to an apartment in Paris's most fashionable district, he owned the island of Skorpios, off the coast of Greece. He and Jackie were married there, Jackie's children with her. Her sister, Lee, was once again her matron of honor.

On Skorpios, Caroline had her own pony and John Jr., a speedboat. The children spent summers there but continued

Much of the world was surprised and dismayed when she married Onassis.

their schooling in Manhattan. Jackie had moved to New York after JFK's assassination, shielding her children from the press while attempting to find normalcy. Caroline had play dates with friends and John often accompanied Jackie to the gym. She kept their father's memory alive, taking them to Acapulco, where she and JFK had honeymooned, and to his ancestral home of Ireland.

Jackie Onassis continued to stay in New York while her children were in school there. Her second marriage, meanwhile, was far from idyllic. Earthy and prone to vulgarity, Onassis was far too coarse for his refined wife. In response to a question about her reason for marrying Onassis, Jackie told a reporter for an Athens newspaper shortly after Onassis died in 1975, "Aristotle Onassis rescued me at a moment when my life was engulfed with shadows." After his death, Jackie returned to the United States full time and became a literary editor for two major New York publishers. Once again, she applied her hands-on devotion to something she cherished.

Her contributions toward preserving American culture and history are seen not only in the rooms of the White House that she so fastidiously restored, but also in the John F. Kennedy Center for the Performing Arts in Washington—the realization of a dream for a national cultural center; in the JFK Presidential Library and Museum in Boston, which succeeds in being both uplifting and contemplative; and in the magnificent Art Deco masterpiece of Grand Central Station in New York, whose demolition Jackie was instrumental in stopping.

She returned only once to the White House after JFK's death, for a private viewing in 1971 of the official portraits of her husband and herself. In a gesture that speaks to the civility of politics in that era, it was First Lady Pat Nixon, the wife of then-President Richard Nixon, whom JFK had defeated in 1960, who invited Jackie and the children to see the por-

Many years later, Jackie's daughter, Caroline, said, she had a "second act" after being wife and mother.

traits. Aaron Shikler painted both—Jackie looking ethereal and gazing off to the side, JFK looking down, arms folded; appearing deep in thought.

Jackie spent the remainder of her life in quiet, intellectual pursuits and devoted to her children. She died on May 19, 1994, of lymphoma, surrounded by her family in her New York City home. She was sixty-four. It fell to John Jr. to announce his mother's death to the media. In a different kind of salute from the one to his father thirty years before, he said of his mother: "She did it in her own way and on her own terms and we all feel lucky for that." He was speaking of the manner in which Jacqueline Bouvier Kennedy Onassis died. But he could just as easily have been describing the way she had lived.

Kennedy Jacqueline
Jacqueline Kennedy
Kennedy Jacqueline
Jacqueline Kennedy
Kennedy Jacqueline
Jacqueline Kennedy
Kennedy Jacqueline
Jacqueline Kennedy
Kennedy Jacqueline
Jacqueline Kennedy
Kennedy Jacqueline
Jacqueline Kennedy